NARCISSISTIC TRAPS

BREAKING FREE FROM ABUSE, GASLIGHTING, TRAUMA BONDS, AND THE PATTERNS THAT KEEP YOU STUCK

SHARELLE ELLIS

NARCISSISTIC TRAPS

Breaking Free From Abuse, Gaslighting, Trauma Bonds, and the Patterns that Keep You Stuck

Copyright © 2026 Sharelle Ellis

ISBN: 979-8-9941688-6-8

Book Design by Transcendent Publishing

Editing by Dana Micheli

This book is for educational and informational purposes only. It is not intended to replace professional psychological, medical, or legal advice. Any resemblance to real individuals, events, or situations is coincidental or used with permission. Readers should seek licensed professionals for support regarding abuse, trauma, mental health, or legal matters.

Printed in the United States of America.

*Something did not feel right long before you
had language for it.*

TABLE OF CONTENTS

This book is dedicated to Mrs. Vanessa, the mother I chose with my heart before I had the words for what I needed. Thank you for standing beside me when my world felt unstable, for believing in my healing when I could not yet believe in myself, and for reminding me that safety can exist again.

I also dedicate this book to the domestic violence programs and advocates who helped me find my footing. Your protection, patience, and resources gave me space to breathe, to think clearly, and to begin again.

And finally, this book is for every woman who has ever questioned her reality in silence. May these pages meet you where you are.

LETTER TO THE READER

Dear Love,

I want to speak to you plainly and honestly. You have lived through something that altered you, even if you did not have language for it at the time. If you are here, it is because something in you is still paying attention to who you really are and what you deserve.

This book is not written to correct you or to move you toward a conclusion. It exists because some experiences are difficult to name while they are happening, and even harder to explain afterward.

As you read the following pages, you may notice responses that arrive quietly or unexpectedly. You are not expected to move through this book quickly or continuously. You may pause, step away, or return later whenever you need to. Read in the way that feels most supportive to you.

My hope is that as you read, you recognize yourself in ways that feel grounding rather than overwhelming, and that you feel less alone with what you remember.

With care,
Sharelle

PRAYER FOR YOUR JOURNEY

We hold in our thoughts every person carrying the weight of abuse. You see the injuries that are visible and the ones that are not. You remain present with what was endured.

Offer steadiness where fear still lives. Restore calm where disruption has taken hold. Let those who feel alone experience moments of safety and recognition.

Bring supportive people into their lives, including listeners, advocates, and communities that understand. Help rebuild what was damaged, gently and without urgency.

For those seeking justice, guide their steps with clarity. For those still silent, allow light to reach them in ways they can bear.

PROLOGUE

The Beautiful Monster

He did not walk into my life. He invaded it, like a disease wearing a human face, a beautiful infection that slid beneath my skin and called itself love. No one ever tells you that monsters wear cologne and smile like safety, or that their words drip sweetness while their intentions carry harm.

In the beginning, he was dazzling and magnetic. He felt impossible to resist. He studied vulnerabilities with precision, memorized every one, and mirrored back a version of myself I wanted to believe was real. I felt chosen, though I did not yet understand that I was being marked.

A narcissist offers rescue while quietly planning control. He elevates you until you surrender, then reshapes the ground beneath you. My laughter became information. My peace became a challenge. Every compliment carried conditions, and every silence felt weighted with threat.

Narcissists observe. They catalogue. They learn where the pressure points are and know just how much force to apply. Their affection is a tool and their withdrawal is a punishment. Everything is part of their agenda, slowly erasing the person you were before the distortion began.

When it ended, there was no dramatic collapse, but it did leave a great deal of residue. I found no pieces that could be easily gathered, but something finer and harder to name. What once felt like destiny revealed itself as the force that nearly dismantled my sense of self. The question that followed lingered long after he was gone: How could something that felt so convincing cause so much harm?

A NOTE BEFORE YOU BEGIN

This book is not meant to be read quickly or consumed in a single emotional pass. Some parts may feel immediately familiar, while others may not make sense until later. That is normal.

You may recognize yourself in ways that arrive quietly rather than all at once. You may feel clarity in one chapter and confusion in the next. You may pause, reread, or skip sections entirely. None of that means you are doing this wrong.

This book does not ask you to decide anything about your past, your relationship, or yourself. It does not require agreement. It does not demand conclusions. It simply offers language for experiences that are often difficult to name while they are happening.

Some readers notice physical responses before emotional ones. Others recognize patterns before they recognize their feelings. Some feel relief. Others feel discomfort. All of these responses are valid.

You do not need to remember everything you read here. You do not need to apply it immediately. Understanding often continues after the reading stops.

If at any point you need to step away, you can. If you need to move slowly, you should. This book will still be here when you return.

WHAT THIS BOOK IS NOT

This book is not a diagnostic manual, and it does not attempt to label or clinically define anyone in your life. It does not ask you to assign motives, defend your choices, or prove what happened to you.

It is not written to rush healing or to frame endurance as strength. It does not suggest that insight arrives all at once or that understanding automatically brings closure.

This book does not ask you to forgive, reconcile, or reinterpret harm in order to feel at peace. It does not offer affirmations, instructions, or steps to follow. It does not promise resolution by the final page.

It also does not assume that leaving was simple, that staying was foolish, or that clarity should have come sooner. Survival required adaptation, and adaptation often happens without conscious choice.

This book is meant to stay with the internal experience of confusion, attachment, and gradual recognition. It offers language, not direction. It makes space for understanding to unfold at its own pace.

CHAPTER ONE

THE SUBTLE SHIFT: WHEN YOU REALIZE SOMETHING IS WRONG

The realization rarely arrives as a single, dramatic moment. It more often takes shape as a quiet awareness that something no longer aligns with what you are being told. The relationship may still look functional from the outside. There may still be moments of connection or affection. Beneath them runs a steady current of unease. You begin to notice small inconsistencies, subtle shifts in tone, and reactions that feel disproportionate or confusing. Nothing is overt enough to name, yet everything feels slightly off.

This early stage is where many survivors struggle most, because while there have been signs of harm, it has not yet become undeniable. The mind searches for explanations that preserve stability, while the body responds with tension, vigilance, and fatigue. You may dismiss these reactions as stress, sensitivity, or overthinking, especially if the person in front of you insists that nothing is wrong. Still, the sense of dissonance persists. Something is happening that you cannot fully articulate, but you can feel it shaping the atmosphere of the relationship.

This chapter examines that first internal fracture, the point at which intuition begins to surface despite confusion, and the subtle signals that mark the beginning of psychological distortion. Before gaslighting becomes explicit and before control hardens into patterns, there is often a period where awareness flickers in and out. Understanding this phase matters, because it is where many survivors later realize that the truth was present long before they had language for it.

Most survivors do not recognize the shift immediately. They instead describe a feeling that is subtle, disorienting, and easily dismissed. There is a slight coldness where warmth once lived, a tone that feels sharper without explanation. There is a sense that something important has changed, though nothing obvious has happened.

The man you thought you knew does not disappear all at once. Instead, he becomes inconsistent. Affection is offered and withdrawn without warning. Kindness is replaced with irritation. You are left trying to figure out what you did wrong, because the version of him you bonded to still exists, just enough to keep you hoping. This is not accidental. When the mask begins to crack, it is rarely dramatic. It is subtle enough that you question yourself rather than him. You tell yourself he is stressed, tired, or misunderstood. You believe that if you are just a little more patient, a little more careful, and a little more understanding, things will return to how they were. That belief is powerful, and it is exactly what keeps the trap intact.

What is happening beneath the surface is a psychological shift. The consistency that once made you feel safe is replaced with unpredictability. Your nervous system begins scanning for cues. You become alert to changes in mood, tone, and energy. You are no longer relaxed inside the relationship. You are managing it. Again, few survivors can identify the moment the conditioning first began. That is not because they missed something obvious, but because of the nature of narcissistic abuse. It begins with comfort that is subtly and systematically stripped away.

In the earliest stage, the connection feels unusually intense, affirming, and aligned. Conversations move quickly into emotional depth. Compliments feel specific and personal. The bond feels rare, even fated. You may feel seen in a way that feels long overdue, as though someone finally recognizes parts of you that have always gone unnoticed.

Narcissistic personalities rely on rapid emotional closeness because speed bypasses discernment. When intimacy accelerates faster than trust can form, your nervous system bonds before your mind has time to evaluate patterns. This does not happen because you are naïve or desperate. It happens because you are human.

At this stage, information is being gathered. Your compassion, values, boundaries, and past wounds are carefully observed. What brings you joy, what triggers guilt, what you tolerate, and what you fear losing are all noted. This is the narcissist's way of establishing leverage, but it looks a lot like nurturing closeness. That makes this phase so disorienting; in fact, many survivors describe it as one of the happiest of their lives. That memory later becomes part of the trauma bond, making it harder to leave when the dynamic begins to shift.

As time passes, small changes appear. Compliments become conditional. Attention fluctuates, with subtle dismissals followed by affection. You may notice a feeling of relief when that happens, and/or that you're working harder to regain the ease that once felt effortless. This is where self-doubt quietly enters. Instead of questioning the behavior, you begin questioning yourself. You wonder if you are being too sensitive, too demanding, or just "too much." This is the beginning of psychological control. By the time confusion becomes distress, the emotional bond is already formed. The thought of leaving is destabilizing, even devastating. And that is the trap functioning exactly as designed.

You remember the beginning because it felt meaningful, affirming, and almost sacred. It felt like being chosen. It felt like being seen beyond appearances. He seemed to notice not the version of yourself you performed for the world, but the quieter parts you kept hidden, and he admired those parts. He made you believe the qualities you once doubted were actually your greatest strengths. That is why the next phase hurts so deeply.

The truth does not arrive as a dramatic event. It arrives slowly and carefully, almost as if it does not want to wake you. What survivors rarely say out loud is this: you feel the truth before you understand it. Your body recognizes danger first. Your spirit begins to lean away. Something inside you knows what your mind is not yet ready to accept.

When the Body Knows Before the Mind Understands

Long before language forms around the experience, the body responds. Many survivors recall feeling unsettled without being able to explain why. Tension appears in the shoulders. Tightness settles in the chest. Unease lingers, even during moments that appear calm on the surface. These are actually intuitive signals. The trauma caused by a narcissist rarely, if ever, begins with a single, obvious incident. It is usually the gradual erosion of clarity, trust, and emotional safety. Your body responds to that erosion even when your mind is still searching for explanations that preserve the relationship.

When confusion replaces certainty, the nervous system shifts into vigilance. You may begin monitoring his moods, choosing words carefully, and anticipating reactions before they occur. This constant adjustment is exhausting. Over time, it teaches you to prioritize emotional survival over self-expression. Understanding this normal human response reframes the story you may have been telling yourself. You did not miss the signs because you were foolish. You felt them. You simply did not yet have the language or support to trust what your body already knew.

Every survivor can point to a turning point, even if it did not feel significant at the time. Again, it usually arrives as discomfort, a quiet resistance in the body. Awakening to the truth is rarely graceful. It often requires a level of honesty that feels destabilizing at first. As clarity begins to form, you start seeing the relationship as a whole rather than as a series of isolated moments. You recognize the carefully engineered beginning, the gradual shift, the confusion, and the harm. You also begin to see how much of yourself you sacrificed in order to survive within the dynamic.

At some point, the realization settles in. What you believed was love was conditioning. What you believed was a connection was control. What you endured was harm presented as gentleness.

HOW NARCISSISTS TARGET STRONG WOMEN

One of the most damaging misconceptions surrounding narcissistic abuse is the belief that it happens because a woman is weak, naïve, or incapable of recognizing warning signs. In reality, many survivors later come to realize they were targeted precisely because of their strength. They were emotionally intelligent, empathetic, resilient, independent, and capable of holding complexity. These qualities are not deficiencies. In healthy relationships, they create intimacy, mutual respect, and stability. In narcissistic dynamics, they become points of access.

A narcissist does not experience strength the way a healthy partner does. Where a grounded partner sees strength as something to honor and meet, a narcissist sees it as something to extract from and exploit. A strong woman reflects well on him. She enhances his image, absorbs emotional strain, and often carries the relationship through moments when it should collapse. Her depth becomes his resource. Her endurance becomes his permission.

This targeting is not accidental. It is strategic.

Empathy is often mistaken for softness, but it is a form of emotional intelligence. Empathetic women perceive nuance, tolerate discomfort, and respond with compassion even in difficult situations. These qualities foster deep connection in healthy relationships. In narcissistic ones, they are manipulated. A narcissist learns quickly that empathy can be leveraged. He shares stories that elicit concern. He presents himself as misunderstood, wounded, or unfairly treated by others. Past relationships are framed to position him as the victim. Each explanation invites understanding. Each justification invites patience. Each apology invites forgiveness without repair. Over time, compassion can shift into self-abandonment, not because the woman lacks boundaries, but because she has been subtly encouraged to prioritize understanding over self-protection.

Independence presents a similar paradox. Many survivors were capable decision-makers before the relationship began. They trusted their judgment, managed their lives, and supported themselves emotionally and practically. While this independence may initially attract a narcissist, it ultimately threatens his need for control. To resolve this tension, independence is slowly undermined. Decisions are questioned. Confidence is eroded. Help is offered that later becomes leverage. Autonomy is reframed as a flaw rather than a strength. What he is reacting to is not independence itself, but his discomfort with not being essential. Abuse comes in many forms. The absence of scars, black eyes, or visible injuries does not mean harm was absent. Abuse can be mental, emotional, or verbal, and it often occurs in ways that are difficult to recognize while they are happening. Loyalty is often misused in the same way. In healthy relationships, loyalty grows from consistency, care, and mutual respect. In narcissistic dynamics, loyalty is exploited. Strong women often take commitment seriously. They do not leave at the first sign of difficulty. They believe in working through challenges and honoring emotional investment. A narcissist recognizes this and uses it to extend the relationship far beyond the point where it remains safe. Love becomes endurance. Commitment becomes self-sacrifice. Loyalty becomes permission to continue causing harm.

These signals rarely arrive loudly. They appear quietly, disguised as affection, insecurity, or intensity. Long before overt abuse becomes visible, the nervous system senses that something is wrong.

Control frequently enters the relationship under the name of love. It may begin with jealousy that feels overwhelming rather than flattering. A partner may demand constant attention, become angry when you spend time with others, or frame possessiveness as devotion. Over time, this need for access expands. Comments about what you wear, where you go, who you speak to, and how much time you owe him begin to shape your daily life. Gradually, the dynamic shifts. You stop feeling like an equal partner and begin to feel like something that belongs to him.

All-consuming jealousy is not a sign of passion. It is a sign of entitlement. When a person expects your attention at all hours, reacts with anger when you prioritize other relationships, or insists on monitoring how you spend your time, the relationship moves from connection into control. The lived experience of the partner on the receiving end is not closeness, but confinement. The earliest warning signs of this dynamic are often felt in the body long before the mind can fully articulate them.

Isolation follows closely behind. Slowly and deliberately, the abuser pulls you away from family, friends, and anyone who might offer perspective or protection. The people you love are criticized. Conflicts are stirred. Guilt is introduced whenever you attempt to maintain those relationships. Over time, your world narrows until he occupies the center of it. This strategy is not accidental. Isolation weakens external support and strengthens dependency.

When complete isolation is not possible, the narcissist uses criticism to drive a wedge between you and your support system. Family members are portrayed as toxic. Friends are labeled untrustworthy. Anyone who questions the relationship is framed as a threat. The result is distance, doubt, and a growing sense of being alone, even when others are still physically present in your life.

As control deepens, privacy begins to disappear. Your phone, your messages, and your social media activity are no longer treated as personal. Passwords are demanded. Devices are checked without permission. Questions about your whereabouts become interrogations rather than expressions of care. Boundaries are framed as secrecy. Independence is treated as betrayal. These behaviors are not expressions of concern. They are violations of autonomy.

Excessive texting often plays a central role in this erosion. What initially appears attentive can quickly become intrusive. Constant messages, demands for immediate responses, repeated requests for updates, and accusations of hiding something are all methods of monitoring rather than connecting. A phone meant to connect you to the world becomes a tether that binds you to one person's need for control.

Emotional and verbal abuse often follows. Disrespect is introduced gradually, making it easier to rationalize and harder to name. Insults are delivered as jokes. Criticism is framed as honesty. Humiliation is disguised as concern. Over time, this language reshapes how you see yourself. Name-calling, belittling comments about intelligence or appearance, dismissing your feelings, or blaming you for being too sensitive are not misunderstandings. They are deliberate attempts to erode self-esteem and authority over your own experience.

Blame becomes routine. Since you are positioned as the emotional center of his world, his behavior is explained as a reaction to you. His anger becomes something you caused. His cruelty becomes your responsibility. Accountability is inverted until you are carrying the weight of his actions while he remains untouched by consequence.

As the cycle intensifies, explosive reactions to minor issues create an atmosphere of fear and unpredictability. Yelling, intimidation, destruction of property, cycles of apology followed by repetition, and accusations that you provoked his outbursts train you to anticipate and manage his emotions. You learn to stay quiet, careful, and compliant to avoid triggering the next eruption.

In more severe cases, threats escalate. These may include threats of self-harm, threats toward people you love, destruction of belongings as punishment, tracking your movements, interrogating your whereabouts, or secretly monitoring your location. Fear becomes the mechanism of control. Compliance becomes a survival strategy.

Sexual coercion often emerges within this same pattern of entitlement. Pressure replaces consent. Guilt, manipulation, emotional withdrawal, or threats of abandonment are used to secure access to your body. When refusal is punished and compliance is expected, consent is no longer freely given. It is extracted. Your body is yours. Any dynamic that treats access as an obligation rather than a choice is a violation.

What makes these patterns especially devastating is the way responsibility becomes distorted over time. You may begin to doubt yourself, apologize for things you did not do, and question whether you deserve basic respect. This confusion has nothing to do with your ability to perceive the situation; it is the result of sustained psychological manipulation.

These dynamics are not expressions of love. They are not examples of healthy conflict. They are not misunderstandings that can be resolved through better communication. They are systems of control designed to disorient, diminish, and dominate.

These behaviors reveal a blueprint of control that sharpens with time. You were never meant to shrink yourself to survive someone else's insecurities. You were meant to love and be loved in ways that feel safe, steady, and honoring to who you are.

Many readers recognize themselves in these patterns for the first time here, and that recognition alone can be profoundly stabilizing.

Chapter Two exists to make one truth unmistakably clear. You were not targeted because you lacked strength. You were targeted because you had it.

What follows is the next layer of understanding. Once control is established, reality itself must be reshaped to maintain it. In the next chapter, we examine the psychological mechanism that keeps reality distorted long after the relationship begins to unravel.

Some patterns are easier to recognize in hindsight than they are while they are forming. Strength is often mistaken for safety, both by the person who carries it and by the person who learns how to exploit it. What may feel like resilience can quietly become a reason to endure what should not be endured.

Many women do not recognize targeting as it is happening because it does not arrive as harm. It arrives as attention, admiration, and relief. Only later does it become clear that qualities such as empathy, competence, and emotional depth were not simply appreciated, but studied and used.

Recognition does not always feel like certainty. Sometimes it shows up as a subtle discomfort, a lingering thought, or a quiet sense that something you once admired was also the doorway through which control entered. Noticing that does not change the past, but it can begin to change how you understand yourself within it.

CHAPTER THREE

GASLIGHTING:
THE WAR ON YOUR REALITY

Before You Knew What Was Happening

Before the violence, there was confusion. Before fear took hold, there was self-doubt. Before your body learned to brace, there was guilt. None of this happened all at once. It unfolded quietly, in ways that were difficult to recognize while you were still inside it.

He trained me, not in obedience, but in uncertainty. Over time, I learned to monitor his moods and anticipate his reactions. I learned to apologize for things I hadn't even done. I learned to shrink my voice, my joy, and my boundaries. I learned to question my own memory, even when I was certain of what I had experienced.

He never told me to stop being myself. He didn't have to. He simply made being myself feel unsafe. Slowly, piece by piece, I gave up parts of who I was, believing that would keep the peace. I believed it would bring back the man from the beginning. I did not yet understand that the man from the beginning had never existed.

There were warning signs I was trained to overlook. He talked end-lessly about himself, and I called it "passion." He avoided emotional accountability, and I told myself he was "guarded." He moved quickly, and I labeled it "fate." He described every former partner as unstable, and I felt relieved that I was different. He overwhelmed me with grand gestures, and I interpreted them as generosity rather than manipulation.

These were all signposts, pointing toward a danger I was not yet able to see. When the mask is in place, red flags can appear like invitations.

Over time, the purpose of the mask becomes clearer: to secure your trust before the truth is revealed. The narcissist is not wearing it because they are shy or afraid of intimacy. They are wearing it because if you saw the real them too soon, you would leave.

Narcissists cannot tolerate rejection, so the mask remains in place for as long as necessary. It stays on while they claim your love, your time, your energy, your empathy, your resources, and the light of your spirit. By the time the mask slips, much of the rewiring has already occurred.

Dr. Jekyll and Mr. Hyde:
The Man with Two Faces

It wasn't his cruelty that made him so difficult to understand. It was who he was when he was kind.

There were two versions of him, and they could appear within the same day, sometimes within the same hour. One version was attentive, warm, affectionate, and present. He spoke softly. He listened closely. He made you feel safe, chosen, and deeply connected. His energy was intoxicating. This was the man you bonded to, the man you loved.

The other version arrived without warning.

His tone became cold; his gaze hardened; he physically pulled away. His reactions to something you said or did were disproportionate. You were left trying to understand how the man who had just held you could suddenly feel like a complete stranger.

Like Dr. Jekyll and Mr. Hyde, he lived in extremes, and you never knew which one would walk through the door, answer the phone, or wake up beside you.

When he withdrew or turned cold, you searched for what you had done wrong. When warmth returned, you felt relief rather than alarm.

This cycle creates attachment through instability. You feel like you have to earn his kindness and that you deserve his cruelty. Over time, your nervous system becomes conditioned to chase moments of peace inside chaos.

It may seem that the man with two faces is conflicted, but that's not the case. He is controlling, and his weapon of choice is emotional whiplash. The confusion is the outcome. And your self-doubt is the result.

Power, Control, and the Escalation of Reality Distortion

Gaslighting is a powerful method of control. You learned to read his moods, monitor your words, and adjust your behavior in hopes of keeping the "good" version present. Chronic lying keeps the survivor off balance and dependent on the abuser's version of reality. The survivor learns that clarity leads to conflict, while confusion feels safer.

As control begins to weaken, the behavior escalates. Lies become more frequent. Stories grow more dramatic. Threats may surface, sometimes subtly and sometimes overtly. These threats are not always about physical harm. They may involve reputational damage, financial consequences, abandonment, or self-harm designed to trap the survivor through fear and responsibility.

This escalation is not emotional instability. It is strategy. When control is threatened, the tactics intensify.

The Pattern That Repeats

Over time, a broader pattern often becomes visible. Many survivors later discover that the confusion they lived inside was not isolated to them alone. Similar stories surface. Similar timelines repeat. The same behaviors appear in different places, with different people, under different circumstances.

What once felt intensely personal begins to look patterned. Survivors begin to recognize that they travel around leaving a trail of destruction and broken hearts, not because each relationship failed in a unique way, but because the same dynamics were repeated again and again.

This understanding does not arrive to provoke fear or anger. It arrives quietly, as context. It explains why the damage felt so disproportionate, and why the harm extended beyond a single relationship. What you experienced was not a singular failure of connection, but part of a repeated dynamic that continues wherever distortion and control are allowed to take hold.

Mirror Games

What follows is drawn from lived experience and is not included for dramatic effect, but to illustrate how carefully constructed vulnerability is often rehearsed and deployed.

The mask is not worn to hide the truth. It is worn to make you believe a lie.

The bathroom light buzzed faintly overhead, casting a jaundiced glow across the small, tiled space. He closed the door with care, muffling the latch so the woman sleeping just down the hall would not stir. Her toothbrush rested in its cup.

Her robe dangled from the hook. Her perfume still lingered on the towel. None of it mattered. None of it ever did.

He leaned toward the mirror. The glass had become his stage, and he knew the choreography well. His eyes drooped. His mouth collapsed into a sorrowful frown. He tilted his chin downward as though carrying invisible weights. The transformation was subtle, calculated, and flawless.

The shutter clicked softly.

The man in the photo looked devastated, hollowed out by heart-break. It was a masterpiece of misery. He scrolled to her name, the new supply, his next victim. His fingers flew across the keys, weaving the familiar script.

He wrote that he did not know how much more he could take. He told her that the woman he lived with treated him like he was nothing and that he felt unwanted. He said he was sitting there crying and had never felt so broken. He attached the photo.

The mask of sorrow traveled instantly through the ether and landed in her hands. The phone vibrated. His heart thumped with anticipation. She replied with concern, telling him she hated imagining him hurting and that he did not deserve it. He smirked at the screen.

The hook had landed.

Another message left his fingertips, sharp and convincing. He wrote that she did not even notice him anymore, that he slept in the same bed but felt invisible, and that he did not think he could stay there much longer.

Miles away, under the soft glow of her bedside lamp, the new woman pressed a hand to her chest. She had only known him for weeks, but his sadness felt raw and urgent. She imagined him standing in that bathroom, broken, mistreated, and unseen. Her thumbs moved quickly; her compassion stronger than her caution. She told him he did not have to stay there and that he could come live with her and she would take care of him and love him right.

His smile widened.

The performance was perfected. He glanced at the mirror again, catching the reflection of the predator behind the mask. For a fleeting moment, he wondered if he had overplayed it, if she might notice the recycled words or the repeated script.

Then the phone vibrated again. She told him he did not deserve any of it. She said she could see that he was a good man and that she wanted to be the one to love him the right way.

With that, the curtain fell.

He slipped the phone into his pocket, switched off the light, and padded softly back down the hall. He paused at the bedroom doorway. His current lover lay still, her face serene and trusting. She dreamed in peace, unaware of the betrayal already sealing her fate.

Tomorrow he would vanish, leaving her with nothing but questions and the echo of lies. She was so blinded by his performance, by the sorrow he manufactured, that the new supply could not see the truth. She was not rescuing a broken man. She was stepping into the role of his next victim.

What You Just Witnessed

What you just read was not an isolated event. It's a true story right out of the narcissist's playbook.

Gaslighting works by manufacturing emotional reality. The same stories are reused. The same wounds are presented. The same emotions are staged. Over time, the survivor begins to question their own perception and trusting the abuser's narrative instead.

This is how reality fractures.

Strong women often blame themselves for believing in a façade that later appears obvious. What they do not realize is that the manipulation was rehearsed. It was practiced. It was designed to bypass logic by appealing directly to empathy.

The problem is never your compassion; it's his lack of integrity.

Gaslighting is one of the narcissist's favorite tools of gaining and maintaining control. By destabilizing your sense of reality, the narcissist ensures that you doubt yourself instead of questioning the harm being done to you.

This gradually erodes your sense of self through repeated invalidation, contradiction, and emotional reversal. Over time, you adapt by silencing your own perception in order to survive.

You were not imagining what happened. You were being trained to distrust yourself.

Clarity does arrive, but not all at once. It returns in pieces, through understanding, self-trust, and the willingness to believe your own experience again.

Clarity rarely returns all at once. For many survivors, it emerges gradually, through moments of recognition that arrive after the confusion has already done its work. Understanding may come in fragments, and trust in your own perception often rebuilds more slowly than awareness.

What matters is not how quickly certainty forms, but that doubt no longer points inward. The destabilization you experienced was not a failure of perception. It was the result of sustained distortion applied over time.

As this understanding settles, it becomes possible to see why leaving did not feel simple, even after something felt wrong. What follows is not weakness, but attachment shaped under pressure. That is where the next layer begins.

CHAPTER FOUR

TRAUMA BONDS: WHY LEAVING FEELS IMPOSSIBLE

There comes a point when you realize that what kept you there was not belief in the relationship, but attachment to relief. You were no longer staying because things were good, but for the moments when the tension lifted. When the warmth returned, your body softened. Your breathing slowed. Your thoughts quieted. For a brief moment, you felt safe again. That sensation is powerful. It can feel like love returning. In reality, it is your nervous system settling after distress.

A trauma bond forms when your body begins to associate closeness with survival. The inconsistency becomes the glue. The pain sharpens the relief. The relief strengthens the attachment. Over time, your system learns that separation equals danger, even when staying is what is hurting you. This is why logic alone never breaks the bond. You can understand the abuse. You can name the patterns. You can even say out loud that the relationship is unhealthy. And still, the thought of leaving can make your chest tighten, your stomach drop, and your mind spiral. As mentioned earlier, this has nothing to do with weakness. Your body simply learned the relationship before your mind could question it.

The Hope That Keeps You Attached

Many survivors blame themselves for continuing to hope after the relationship took a negative turn. They ask why they kept believing in change when the evidence said otherwise. What often goes unspoken is that hope is not a flaw. Hope is a survival strategy. Hope allows the mind to endure what the body is already carrying. Hope tells you that the pain has a purpose. Hope convinces you that if you can just get back to the beginning, everything will make sense again. But the beginning was not a promise. It was a hook.

The bond strengthens because hope becomes tied to intermittent reward. Each apology, each moment of tenderness, each glimpse of the person you thought he was resets the cycle. Your nervous system registers that return as proof that the connection is still alive. Your body responds before your mind has time to protect you. This is why leaving feels like losing something vital, even when what you are losing has been harming you.

Why Separation Feels Like Withdrawal

When a trauma bond is active, separation from that person feels like loss, panic, and disorientation. You may experience waves of grief that make no sense to others. You may miss the person who hurt you. You may crave contact even when you know it is unsafe. This is not because you want the abuse. It is because your body is recalibrating.

The nervous system does not release attachments all at once. It needs time, consistency, and safety to relearn regulation without chaos. This is why many survivors return—their bodies are seeking the familiar rhythm of tension and relief. Understanding this is critical because it removes moral judgment and shame from your healing.

The Quiet Moment When the Bond Begins to Loosen

There is a moment when something shifts. The pull is still there, but it no longer owns you. As said earlier, this moment is rarely a dramatic one. Rather, it feels calm, almost neutral. The urge to reach out passes instead of consuming you. You notice that your body can settle without waiting for his return. You are getting a taste of freedom.

The bond loosens when safety becomes consistent, when your days are predictable, when your nervous system learns that peace does not have to be earned through pain, and when your body realizes that calm can exist without chaos preceding it. You cannot force yourself to let go of a trauma bond. You loosen it by creating conditions where your body no longer needs it.

If you have felt confused while reading this chapter, that confusion is not a failure to understand. It is a sign that your body recognizes what your mind is still learning how to hold. Trauma bonds form because the nervous system adapts to instability in order to survive it. They have *nothing* to do with weaknesses or lack of awareness.

When love becomes unpredictable, the body does not ask whether it is healthy. It figures out how to survive. It learns the rhythms of tension and relief. It learns to wait for warmth. It learns to hope through discomfort. Over time, that waiting can feel like loyalty, and that hope can feel like devotion. What was happening was conditioning.

Leaving a trauma bond often feels like stepping into free fall. The relationship may have been painful, but it was familiar. The body knew how to function inside it. Separation removes the familiar cues, even when those cues were harmful. That absence can feel like panic, grief, and disorientation all at once. Many survivors interpret that reaction as proof that they made the wrong choice. In truth, it is proof that their nervous system is recalibrating.

There is nothing wrong with you for missing someone who hurt you. There is nothing shameful about feeling pulled back toward what once felt like safety. These sensations are remnants of a bond that once helped you survive something you did not yet know how to escape.

Healing begins by allowing your body to feel safe again. Safety comes through consistency, honesty, and gentleness. It comes through routines that steady you, boundaries that protect you, and relationships that do not require you to disappear in order to be loved.

You do not need to rush this process. You do not need to decide anything today. Awareness alone is movement. Naming what happened loosens its grip. Understanding why leaving felt impossible begins to soften the shame that has kept so many survivors silent.

This chapter is not asking you to let go all at once. It is asking you to stop blaming yourself for what your body did to survive. Compassion is not weakness. It is the beginning of freedom.

Take a moment before moving forward. Notice your breath. Notice the ground beneath you. You are not trapped anymore, even if parts of you still feel afraid. Those parts will learn, slowly and safely, that the danger has passed.

Trauma bonds do not form because someone failed to see the truth. They form because the body learned to associate relief with safety in an environment where distress was constant. What felt like attachment was often the nervous system seeking regulation, not the heart seeking harm.

Many survivors recognize this bond only after leaving, when the intensity remains even without contact. Missing someone who caused pain does not mean the pain was imagined. It means the attachment was conditioned under pressure and reinforced through intermittent relief.

Understanding this does not require immediate separation or resolution. It offers context where there was once shame. It explains why leaving felt impossible without suggesting that staying was a choice made freely. That distinction matters.

CHAPTER FIVE

THE DOUBLE LIFE: LIES, SECRETS, AND HIDDEN BETRAYAL

The most devastating thing for many survivors is the realization that the relationship they believed they were building was never mutual. It was transactional, strategic, and in many cases, being duplicated elsewhere at the same time. A double life is often hidden behind plausible explanations, emotional storytelling, and carefully managed personas. One version of the abuser appears wounded, devoted, and misunderstood. Another version operates in secrecy, extracting resources, attention, and validation wherever they can find it. This chapter is about the moment the illusion collapses. It is about discovering that loyalty was not shared, truth was optional, and love was used as leverage. It is also about the specific cruelty of being blamed for harm you did not cause, while the person who caused it disappears into the next performance.

Reclaiming Yourself: Healing the Identity After Abuse

Most survivors do not realize they are losing themselves while it is happening. Identity erosion is quiet and gradual; it happens through accommodation, silence, and self-correction. You may not remember the exact day you stopped speaking freely. You may not remember when you began filtering your thoughts before sharing them. You may not remember when your preferences began to feel inconvenient, excessive, or unsafe. What you remember instead is a growing sense of absence. Something felt missing, but you could not name what it was. This is how narcissistic abuse dismantles identity, not through force alone, but through conditioning.

How Identity Is Slowly Taken Apart

Narcissists don't say, "Stop being yourself." Instead, they create consequences for authenticity. When you express a need, conflict follows. When you assert a boundary, withdrawal occurs. When you share a feeling, it is dismissed, mocked, or turned against you. Over time, your nervous system learns a painful lesson. Being yourself is risky. Silence feels safer. You may have found yourself minimizing your joy, suppressing your anger, or downplaying your intuition. You may have stopped pursuing interests that once made you feel alive. You may have begun deferring decisions you were once confident making. Each adjustment felt small in isolation, but together they reshaped your identity. You were acting out of survival.

The Difference Between Who You Were and Who You Became

Many survivors struggle with shame when they look back at who they became inside the relationship. They ask why they tolerated things they never thought they would. This shame stems from a misunderstanding of the process. The version of you that existed inside the abuse was not the real you. She was a protective version. She adapted in order to stay emotionally safe. She learned how to survive unpredictability by shrinking, appeasing, or staying quiet. The real you did not disappear. She stepped back so you could endure. Reclaiming yourself means honoring that protective version, then allowing her to rest.

When He Replaces You

It's soul-crushing to see him in a new relationship, especially since it appears perfect. Know that it is not rooted in love, but strategy. The narcissist is working tirelessly to punish you, lure the new woman, save face, rewrite the narrative, present himself as the hero, eliminate suspicion, and avoid accountability. What appears to be intense feelings for this new person is part of his strategy. Beneath it, the same decay that destroyed your relationship is already forming.

The "new supply" is not your competition. She is your mirror. She reflects the woman you once were: hopeful, empathetic, open, trusting, excited, and deeply believing in connection. You and the new supply are more alike than you are different. She is not standing in a better position. She is standing at an earlier point in the same cycle.

She is still inside the glow of the mask, still believing in the story he is selling, still interacting with the version of himself that can be sustained only briefly. She is not better than you. She is not an upgrade. She is simply new, and newness is what fuels the narcissist.

When a narcissist replaces you, the display that follows has nothing to do with love. It is image control—strategic, manipulative, retaliatory, and carefully curated.

The public affection he showers on the new woman is another weapon in his psychological warfare. He wants you to question your memory, your worth, your experience, and your sanity. He wants the world to believe that he was your victim, that he finally found happiness, and that he is capable of love.

Healthy people do not weaponize their new relationships. Only narcissists do.

Seeing this cycle with a new person can trigger the harsh realization every survivor eventually confronts. He did not change for her. He did not become better for her. He simply restarted the cycle with her. It was never about the woman. It was always about the supply.

If she is kind, empathic, loyal, forgiving, hopeful, or emotionally intelligent, then she is exactly the type he seeks, not because those qualities are weaknesses, but because they can be exploited. When the mask cracks, she will find herself exactly where you once stood, confused, isolated, blamed, gaslit, shamed, exhausted, and empty.

The reframe that frees you is this: the new woman is proof only of his repetitive behavior.

You are not witnessing a healthier relationship or his "upgrade." You are witnessing the opening chapter of a story you already survived.

Choosing Yourself Without Apology

Reclaiming your identity means choosing yourself even when it feels unfamiliar. It means trusting your perceptions again. It means allowing your needs to exist without justification. It means honoring the parts of you that were silenced without punishing them. You may still feel grief for what you lost. You may still feel anger for what was taken. Both can coexist with healing. Choosing yourself does not require perfection. It requires honesty. And honesty is what brings you back to yourself.

Narcissistic abuse dismantles identity through emotional conditioning and psychological adaptation. Survivors do not lose themselves because they are weak, but because they are responding to an unsafe environment. Healing begins when you stop competing with illusions and start choosing yourself. The narcissist's new relationship is not a reflection of your worth. It is a repetition of a pattern you survived.

Before You Rebuild Who You Are

Leaving a narcissistic relationship does not immediately return you to yourself. It often leaves you standing in a quiet space where survival has ended, but identity has not yet returned.

You may notice that the urgency is gone, but clarity has not fully arrived. The chaos has quieted, but the mirror feels unfamiliar.

This can feel like failure, but it's not. It is simply the space between.

For so long, your energy was focused on managing someone else: their moods, their reactions, their approval, and their rules.

When that constant pressure disappears, it doesn't always feel freeing—at least, not right away. Many survivors describe this moment as disorienting, not because they miss the person, but because they no longer recognize themselves.

That confusion is actually the first sign that your nervous system is no longer trapped in survival mode.

Before you can build a future, you must meet the woman who remains after survival ends.

Chapter Six is not about becoming someone new. It is about returning to who you were before adaptation replaced authenticity.

Turn the page only when you are ready to meet her.

THE CRASH: WHEN YOUR SOUL FINALLY SAYS ENOUGH

When you finally leave a narcissist, or the narcissistic system that shaped you long before adulthood, you do not walk away as the same woman you were before. You leave cracked open, rearranged, and trying to recognize yourself in the quiet that follows. Identity is the space survivors bleed the most—not the arguments, not the gaslighting, and not even the cruelty. The deepest wound is the loss of self.

Narcissistic abuse is extremely complex; it is a form of possession and psychological hijacking. Over time, it rewrites what you believe about yourself, what you fear, what you tolerate, what you chase, and what you think you deserve. When you finally break free, there is often a silence that feels like a void, a frightening nothingness you do not yet know how to fill.

This chapter begins there. It is where the old identity loosens its grip, and the rebirth quietly starts.

Many survivors are shocked, scared, and devastated when they look at their lives and realize they no longer know what they want. For so long, everything revolved around someone else's moods, rules, punishments, approval, and version of who you were allowed to be. Your identity became a performance and a survival strategy. You learned to shrink, to apologize for existing, to over-explain, to over-function, to anticipate anger, and to prioritize someone else's emotional weather above your own inner truth.

You were trained to dim yourself so they could feel bright. When you begin to break that conditioning slowly, steadily, and with courage, you loosen the identity shaped by survival.

After prolonged trauma, the nervous system (re)organizes itself around adaptation. You may recognize the roles you played while involved with the narcissist: the peacemaker, the fixer, the strong one, the one who endured, or the woman who was always either too much or not enough. These were not reflections of who you truly are. They were protective masks that kept you alive.

When you leave a narcissist, those identities often collapse all at once. What remains can feel disorienting, but it is also a rare and powerful opening. For the first time, you have the chance to rebuild a life based on truth rather than trauma. It reveals itself when you make decisions for your highest good (including saying no) without guilt. These decisions may seem small, but each one is a revolution.

The Return of the Self Happens Slowly

Identity does not return yet; what returns first is quiet. You may notice it when you speak without rehearsing or say no without explaining. You might feel a preference and trust it. Your body starts relaxing instead of bracing. These moments are so important, because they are evidence that your nervous system is learning safety again. **You do not become someone new here. You also do not recover who you were yet. This is the space before identity returns.**

Reclaiming your identity is not optional if you want lasting healing. You cannot build a stable life on a fractured sense of self. You cannot elevate while living from a version of you shaped by survival. You cannot love yourself if you cannot see yourself clearly. Identity is the foundation of boundaries, relationships, self-respect, emotional regulation, life decisions, and purpose. Without it, healing becomes guesswork. With it, healing becomes alignment.

Future Faking: The Promise of a Life They Never Intend To Give

Narcissists are master storytellers. They paint vivid pictures of a beautiful future together, a home, a family, a stable life, not because they intend to build it, but because the fantasy binds you more deeply to them. It is psychological bait, and eventually, the promise becomes a leash.

By the time you realize the future they described was never real, you are already emotionally attached. Hope becomes the tool they use to maintain control.

The reclamation unfolds through four intertwined movements.

The first is reclaiming your voice. Narcissists silence you in thousands of subtle ways before you ever notice the quiet. Reclaiming your voice means allowing yourself to say what you feel, to express what you need, to hold opinions without apology, and to stop softening your presence to make others comfortable.

The second is reclaiming your body. Your body remembers what your mind learned to ignore: the tension, the fear, the shrinking, and the self-erasure. Reclaiming your body has nothing to do with your appearance and everything to do with sovereignty. It looks like breathing deeply again, grounding your nervous system, wearing what feels like you, and allowing yourself to take up space without guilt. Your body is your home, and you are allowed to live in it fully again.

The third is reclaiming your values. During abuse, your values are slowly overwritten by someone else's priorities. Reclaiming them means redis-covering what you believe, what matters to you, and what you refuse to compromise on. These values become your internal compass. They are what make you unmanipulable.

The fourth is reclaiming your future self. She is not just a fantasy or a daydream you have. She is waiting for you to realize the truth of this potential. When you begin orienting your choices toward her, your standards change, your relationships shift, your boundaries solidify, and your life starts moving forward with intention. Your future self becomes your north star.

There is often a moment during this process that feels almost sacred. You may be standing near a window, feeling warmth on your skin, and holding something familiar in your hands. You take a breath, and for the first time in a long while, it reaches all the way down. In that moment, you feel yourself returning—not the woman you were before the abuse or the woman shaped by it, but the woman who always existed underneath survival. You reclaim your identity by leaning into these moments and continuing to make choices that honor who you really are.

If you are reading this chapter and feel unsettled, uncertain, or tender, understand it as evidence that something real is shifting. **Identity is not rebuilt here. It is made possible. This chapter ends before the return begins.**

Leaving does not immediately restore identity. What collapses first is the version of the self that survived by adapting, anticipating, and enduring. The disorientation that follows is not failure or regression. It is the absence of a role that once protected you.

Many survivors mistake this emptiness for loss. In reality, it is space. The nervous system has stepped out of constant threat and has not yet learned what it feels like to exist without bracing. Confusion in this phase is not a sign that leaving was wrong. It is evidence that survival is no longer required in the same way.

This chapter does not complete the return of the self. It marks the moment when survival loosens its grip and identity becomes possible again. What comes next is not reconstruction, but discernment. Clarity will follow when the body no longer has to negotiate for safety.

THE AFTERMATH: WITHDRAWAL, SHAME, AND THE ECHO OF HIS VOICE

When the Mask Fully Falls

There comes a point in the narcissistic relationship when the confusion he causes stops feeling accidental and begins to feel intentional. This is the stage where the mask no longer slips briefly, but fractures. The behaviors you once excused become patterns you can no longer ignore. The secrecy deepens. The lies multiply. The instability escalates. And the man you were told he was no longer matches the man you are living with.

This chapter is about that moment when the double life becomes undeniable, when cheating is no longer just suspected, when secrecy is revealed as strategy, and when control replaces illusion. This is where many survivors finally see the truth clearly, even if leaving still feels impossible.

DL Behavior, Secrecy, and the Double Life

Many narcissistic men live double lives, particularly DL men (also known as "on the down-low," or hiding their homosexuality) who use women as "beards." A beard provides social camouflage. She stabilizes his public image, deflects suspicion, and reassures family, friends, coworkers, and religious communities that he fits the role he wants them to see. When rumors or accusations arise, she is his proof of heterosexuality.

The beard, of course, is unaware of this. She doesn't know why he guards his phone so closely, doesn't share his passwords, or closes screens when she walks in the room. When his secrecy is threatened, he adopts a victim mentality. This allows him to shift blame, earn sympathy, and maintain emotional control.

These men live double lives and wear multiple masks—one for partners, one for others, and one for themselves. Secrecy gives them power. They surround themselves with toxic people because healthy people expose them, while toxic people enable them. Chaos feels safer than accountability.

When the Mask Fully Falls

At this stage, the narcissist is no longer managing perception carefully. His anger escalates more often; he retaliates rather than charms. He also becomes more unstable, often engaging in substance use, reckless behavior, and emotional volatility. The relationship becomes unsafe, unpredictable, and draining.

The takeaway here is that he has not regressed or changed; he has simply revealed who he always was.

Beards are often chosen carefully. Narcissistic and down-low men tend to select women who are empathic, loyal, patient, and protective. These women are more likely to defend him, doubt themselves, and stay quiet when something feels off. Her credibility makes her a better cover.

Over time, the beard is required to perform. She must appear happy. She must support his image. She must remain silent about inconsistencies. If she questions him, she is accused of paranoia. If she confronts him, she is framed as abusive or unstable.

In many cases, the beard is punished for noticing the truth. Emotional withdrawal, gaslighting, infidelity, and sudden cruelty are often attempts to destabilize her confidence so she will stop asking questions.

When the beard is no longer effective, she is discarded. This often happens when she becomes too aware, too vocal, or too strong to manage. The discard is frequently cold and abrupt, because once her role ends, she's no longer relevant to him.

A Deep Dive into Their Psychology

Narcissistic behavior is rooted in emotional immaturity and childish games that persist well into adulthood. This immaturity often shows up through neglecting parental responsibilities, avoiding accountability, and prioritizing personal gratification over duty or care. One of the most powerful mechanisms they use is trauma bonding. Narcissists create trauma bonds through cycles of affection, rejection, reassurance, and cruelty. This cycle functions as the emotional equivalent of addiction and keeps partners psychologically attached even when harm is clear.

Narcissists pursue instant gratification. They live in the present moment and crave sex, attention, praise, power, stimulation, and admiration. Long-term stability does not sustain them. They are emotionally unavailable. Their hearts are locked behind iron gates, not because they do not want intimacy, but because they fear it. Emotional closeness threatens to expose their wounds, their shame, and their emptiness.

Third-party situations and reckless behavior give them power, leverage, chaos, entertainment, and ego boosts. They use and discard people once a person no longer feeds their ego, often doing so coldly, quickly, and cruelly. They enjoy the chase. Being pursued confirms their superiority. Once there is a commitment, however, they lose interest and seek a new high.

Pathological lying is central to the narcissist's behavior. They lie to avoid accountability, gain admiration, manipulate narratives, and craft illusions. Over time, they often begin to believe their own fiction. They have guarded hearts and fear change, because change requires self-reflection and self-reflection requires confronting flaws. As a result, they remain emotionally, mentally, and spiritually stuck. They may grow older, but they never grow up.

The narcissist views life as a game of domination, manipulation, leverage, and winning. People are pawns and empathy is a weakness. Winning is everything. They keep multiple options because commitment feels like a cage. One partner cannot sustain their need for constant admiration.

Their desires are insatiable. Success, money, partners, and attention never fill the emptiness they carry, yet they expect others to fill it. Destructive behavior follows. They destroy relationships, careers, friendships, finances, and families to maintain control or avoid shame. If they cannot dominate something, they sabotage it.

They engage in delusional thinking to protect a fragile ego. Understanding the role of the beard is critical because it clarifies something survivors often blame themselves for. You were not rejected because you were inadequate. You were released because you were no longer useful as cover. In their constructed reality, they are always the hero, always right, always wronged, and always justified. When manipulation stops working, escalation begins. Mental abuse, physical abuse, cruelty, violence, and silence become tools and punishments.

One of the most powerful mechanisms they use is trauma bonding. Narcissists create trauma bonds through cycles of affection, rejection, reassurance, and cruelty. This hot and cold behavior keeps partners addicted, always chasing highs to escape lows.

TEN YEARS TO NOWHERE

A true story. A warning. And a resurrection.

Part I: The Devil You Don't See

He walked into Maya's life wearing a smile that looked comforting and familiar. Adam was polished; his eyes were sharp and assessing, yet he carried himself with the wounded posture of a man who claimed he had survived too much. He spoke gently. He quoted scripture. He wiped tears while telling stories about his difficult childhood. He said he needed a fresh start. He said he needed Maya.

And Maya, who was tender-hearted and trusting, let him in with the belief that she was helping someone who had been hurt.

She did not know that Adam was not broken in the way he pretended to be. He was calculated. He was a shapeshifter. He was a man who moved through women's lives with a routine so practiced that it had almost become an art form. He sought out empathy. He targeted softness. He studied vulnerability the way some people study history.

Maya was not the first. And she was not meant to be the last.

Part II: The Puppeteer

He moved into her life with the speed of a man who had done it many times before. He said the woman he lived with was toxic and he needed somewhere safe to stay. Maya, believing him, opened her door.

Within weeks, he was sleeping in her bed, using her car, and eating her food. He pretended to be looking for work, but Maya paid for the groceries, the gas, the bills, and the rent. She thought she was building a future with someone who simply needed time to get on his feet.

While she held the relationship together, he was tearing it apart in secret.

He used her car to meet lovers, both men and women. He invited strangers into her home and into her bed. He treated her life like a stage where he could perform without consequence. When she confronted him with evidence she did not want to believe, he did not deny anything. He laughed.

"If you don't have proof," he said, "then it never happened."

She stood there shaking, realizing that the man she had opened her heart and her home to was not a partner. He was an emotional thief. He was a man who enjoyed watching her crumble.

Part III: The Isolation Trap

When she tried to reclaim her dignity and leave, Adam shifted. He cried. He begged. He told her he would end his life if she abandoned him.

"Let's move," he said desperately. "We can start over. I will become the man you deserve. I promise I will change."

Maya sacrificed everything.

She sold the home she owned. It belonged to her alone. She sold her car. She sold her furniture. She left her family. She boarded a train with him that took three days to reach a new state where she knew no one. On the entire journey, she kept telling herself that maybe this was their chance to rewrite the story.

But the promise was a lie.

The moment they arrived; he disappeared into the version of himself; she feared most. He refused to work. He slept all day. He played video games for hours. She was stranded in a city where she had no support, no transportation, and no safety net.

After one argument, he walked out of the apartment and out of the state. He left her with no money, no help, and no idea how to survive.

Part IV: The Final Knife

Five days later, Maya's phone lit up with a message from Adam.

"I'm in love now. She's everything you're not. I'm finally happy. Don't contact me again."

She was still legally married to him.

She'd still believed, somewhere deep inside, that the affectionate version of him she met in the beginning had been real. Now the message shattered what remained of that belief.

She told him she was facing eviction. She had no food. She needed help.

His response was short and cold.

"Not my problem. Go to a shelter. Or go back to where you came from. Either way, don't call me again."

Then he blocked her as if ten years had meant nothing. As if she had meant nothing.

Part V: The Devil's Trail

With time and distance, Maya learned she was not alone. There were other women. Dozens of them. Women who carried their own versions of her story.

Adam had children in multiple states; some abandoned before they were even born. He left women dealing with eviction notices, unpaid bills, threats, and heartbreak. He carried untreated infections from partner to partner. He led secret relationships with men. He spent years cycling from one woman to the next, leaving destruction behind him the way a storm leaves broken branches.

He was not a partner. He was a monster wearing human skin.

Part VI: The Resurrection

Maya ended up in a women's shelter during winter, standing in line with a small suitcase and a heart that felt like it could no longer carry its own weight. But pain has a way of clearing the fog that love once created.

She rose.

She found work. She learned the vocabulary of abuse, including gaslighting, trauma bonding, and coercive control. She realized that nothing she endured was a reflection of her value. She learned that Adam had never been capable of love. She learned that her empathy was not a weakness. It was her strength.

She eventually built a life that looked nothing like the one she had escaped. She spoke at survivor events. She helped other women find their voices. She bought her own home. She painted the walls in colors that felt like safety. She rebuilt her life with gentleness and purpose.

She lived near the ocean. She slept without fear. She laughed again, and this time her joy belonged only to her.

She resurrected herself from the ashes he left behind.

Chapter Seven exposes the structure beneath the chaos. DL behavior, secrecy, cheating, and double lives are not isolated traits. They are part of a psychological system built on control, gratification, and avoidance of accountability. The risk to your emotional, psychological, and physical health was intentional and strategic.

By this point in the journey, confusion no longer defines your experience. You can see escalation for what it is: a response to lost control rather than unresolved pain. You can recognize retaliation for what it represents: an attempt to punish autonomy.

This recognition changes everything, but it does not complete the work. Clarity alone does not create safety. Understanding the pattern does not prevent attempts to re-enter your life.

What comes next is learning how to protect yourself without guilt, without over-explaining, and without abandoning your own nervous system in the process. This is where boundaries begin to take shape, not as ultimatums or defenses, but as lived self-respect.

The next chapter is not about them.

It is about you.

When the mask fully falls, clarity can feel unsettling rather than relieving. Seeing the truth does not immediately quiet the body or erase the echo of his voice. Awareness often arrives alongside grief for what was believed, endured, or hoped for, even after the illusion is gone.

What becomes clear in this phase is not simply what he did, but how consistently your reality was overridden in service of control. Recognizing that pattern does not require reliving it or assigning meaning to every detail. It allows you to stop questioning whether your experience was real.

This chapter does not ask you to confront or resolve anything. It marks the point where confusion gives way to recognition, and where your attention begins to shift from deciphering his behavior to protecting your own. That shift is not sudden or dramatic. It is quiet, and it is stabilizing.

CHAPTER EIGHT

RECLAIMING YOURSELF: RESTORING IDENTITY AFTER ABUSE

There is a moment that arrives quietly, without ceremony, when you realize you are no longer orienting your life around someone else's reactions. It does not feel dramatic. It does not feel victorious. It feels unfamiliar in a way that is almost neutral. For the first time in a long while, you are not bracing. You are not anticipating. You are not scanning for consequences.

This is often mistaken for emptiness, but it is not emptiness. It is space.

For a long time, your identity was shaped by proximity. Who you were depended on who you were with, how they felt, and what they needed from you. You learned to measure yourself through their moods, their approval, and their version of reality. When that system disappears, there is a period where nothing rushes in to replace it. The quiet can feel unsettling because it is not yet filled with you.

This is not the return of identity yet. It is the end of being shaped by reaction. Reclaiming yourself begins only after survival stops telling you who you need to be.

Many survivors expect identity to return as a revelation, a decisive moment where everything clicks back into place. That expectation is shaped by survival stories that promise transformation through intensity. What actually happens is slower. Identity returns through ordinary choices that no longer require justification. It returns when your preferences stop feeling negotiable. It returns when your body no longer tightens at the sound of your own voice.

At first, this return can feel disorienting. You may notice that you do not know what you want to eat, how you want to spend your time, or what feels meaningful to you now. This is not a failure of healing. It is evidence that your inner life was interrupted long enough that it needs time to come back online.

You were not indecisive. You were overruled.

When your reality has been shaped by someone else's dominance, your sense of self does not disappear. It goes quiet. It learns to wait. It stops offering input because it was punished for doing so. **Reclaiming yourself begins by allowing that voice to exist without asking it to decide anything yet.**

There is often grief here. Not only for what was taken, but for the version of yourself that adapted in order to survive. You may feel anger toward the woman you became. You may feel embarrassment when you remember how small you felt, how much you tolerated, or how far you drifted from your values. That anger misunderstands the function of adaptation.

You did not become someone else because you were weak. You became someone else because you were enduring.

The version of you that existed inside the abuse was not broken. She was strategic. She learned when to speak and when to stay quiet. She learned how to read danger and minimize fallout. She did not disappear. She stepped aside. Reclaiming yourself does not require rejecting her. It requires allowing her to rest.

As identity returns, it does so unevenly. Some days you may feel grounded and clear. Other days you may feel detached or uncertain. This fluctuation does not mean you are regressing. It means your nervous system is learning that consistency does not have to be earned through vigilance.

You begin to notice moments where you no longer explain yourself. You stop filling silence. You choose rest without guilt. You feel irritation without apologizing for it. These moments are not personality changes. They are corrections.

Reclaiming yourself is not about becoming louder or stronger or more resilient. It is about becoming accurate. Accurate to your limits. Accurate to your values. Accurate to your internal signals.

This accuracy changes how you relate to the world. You may notice that some relationships no longer fit. You may feel less willing to smooth over discomfort or accommodate confusion. This is not coldness. It is clarity returning to its rightful place.

There is often fear here, too. Fear that choosing yourself will make you unlovable. Fear that boundaries will lead to abandonment. Fear that if you stop performing, there will be nothing left to offer. These fears are remnants of a system that rewarded self-erasure.

You are not losing connection by reclaiming yourself. You are losing distortion.

Identity does not return so that you can prove anything. It returns so that you can live without constantly checking whether you are allowed to exist as you are. This is not reinvention. This is remembrance.

You are not becoming someone new. You are no longer organizing yourself around distortion.

Reclaiming yourself does not mean feeling certain, confident, or whole all at once. It means no longer arranging your inner life around distortion. What returns first is not clarity, but permission. Permission to pause, to not know, and to let your preferences re-emerge without pressure.

If this chapter feels quiet rather than empowering, that is not a sign that nothing is happening. It is evidence that survival is no longer directing your attention. The self does not announce its return. It becomes audible again when it is no longer being overridden.

This chapter marks the shift from reacting to remembering. What follows is not transformation, but steadiness. Identity does not need to be rebuilt. It needs space to exist without interference.

CHAPTER NINE

WHAT HEALTHY LOVE IS

Learning To Value You

After prolonged confusion, healthy love often feels unfamiliar before it feels good. Abuse does not only cause pain. It distorts reference points. It teaches the body to associate intensity with connection and instability with passion.

The purpose of this chapter is to illustrate the differences between healthy love and abuse.

For many readers, this chapter marks the beginning of a shift in how they understand themselves.

Healthy love feels steady, calm, and safe. It does *not* bring confusion or chaos; there is no emotional guesswork required. It does not punish you for needing reassurance or clarity. It does not make you feel anxious, hypervigilant, or responsible for managing another adult's emotional state.

Power and Control Versus Love

In abusive dynamics, control is maintained through fear, instability, and confusion. Chronic lying keeps the survivor off balance. Mood swings create emotional dependency. Threats, whether overt or subtle, are used to stifle autonomy.

Threats do not always sound violent. Sometimes they sound like abandonment or even self-harm. Sometimes they involve damage to your reputation or finances. Regardless of the form, the goal is always the same: compliance through fear.

Love does not need leverage. Love does not require you to stay silent to keep the peace. Love does not escalate when questioned. Love does not punish you for autonomy.

Many survivors struggle with this realization because abusive relationships often begin with intensity. Intensity feels powerful, like this is a meant-to-be connection. Over time, this hardwires your body and mind to believe that if it's not present, it's boring. That's not true. In fact, intensity without consistency is not love. It is stimulation.

Peace is the true indicator.

When you are with someone healthy, your body does not brace. Your chest does not tighten before conversations. Your stomach does not drop when your phone vibrates. You are not scanning for tone shifts or preparing for emotional consequences. Your nervous system rests.

There comes a point in healing where you realize all the ways in which the relationship harmed you. It stole pieces of your worth one moment at a time until you began to internalize the feeling that something in you was fundamentally flawed. Before you go any further, I want you to hold this truth gently.

You were never too much. You were never too sensitive. You were never difficult to love. You were simply giving your heart to someone who refused to hold it kindly.

This chapter is about reclaiming the love you gave so freely to others and learning to offer it, fully and without apology, to yourself. After experiencing narcissistic abuse, one of the most profound steps in healing is relearning your inherent value as a person. Yes, the narcissist's conditioning has seeded doubt and shame into your life, but that is not where your story ends.

This chapter is your turning point. This is the moment you choose you.

The Illusion of Unworthiness

For many survivors, unworthiness becomes a quiet undercurrent beneath every thought. It shapes decisions and influences relationships. Narcissistic abuse thrives on that illusion. It teaches you that love must be earned. It convinces you that your needs are annoying, unrealistic, and unfair. It conditions you to depend on the very person who is diminishing you.

Your worth has never been conditional. More importantly, it was never theirs to define.

Understanding this truth takes time. It begins by noticing where you placed your worth. It begins by noticing how often you apologized for existing. Healing invites you to call your value back home.

What Self-Love Is

Self-love is more than a practice. It is the decision, made over and over again, to treat yourself with compassion, regardless of another's cruelty and how you may have internalized it. Self-love is also allowing yourself to rest without guilt. It is choosing boundaries that protect your spirit. It is acknowledging your pain without letting it narrate your entire story.

Examples of self-love include saying no without explanation, leaving situations that require you to abandon yourself, feeding your body with intention, forgiving yourself for what you did not know, trusting the voice that whispered the truth to you when you were not ready to hear it, letting tears fall without shame, and holding your own hand through uncertainty.

Self-love is sacred. It is also essential for survival and rebirth.

Steps to Reclaim Your Self-Worth

Listen to the voice you use when you speak to yourself. Does it carry the tone of the narcissist? Does it echo the dismissiveness or the criticism you endured? Awareness is the first step in reclaiming compassion for yourself. For example:

Old voice: "I should have known better."

New voice: "I did the best I could with what I understood. I am learning, and I am growing."

Many survivors carry beliefs that were given to them long before the abuse began. Beliefs like, "I am not enough," "If I speak up, people will leave," and "I must earn love to deserve it." Ask yourself where each belief came from. Ask if it is true. Ask if it belongs to you.

Rewrite them gently. "I am enough exactly as I am." "My voice matters." "Love does not require my suffering."

Worthiness is strengthened through repetition and ritual. Mirror work involves speaking one truth to yourself each morning. Affirmation journaling involves writing words that build your confidence and self-love using positive words and in the present tense. Celebration lists involve noticing one thing each day that reflects growth. Protecting your peace involves walking away from anything that drains your spirit.

Your peace is not a luxury. It is foundational.

Healing as a Return to Self

Healing is returning to the person you were before life taught you to doubt yourself. It is remembering the child who danced freely, the young woman who loved without fear, and the strength inside you that never left.

Healing is rewriting your story, from broken to becoming. You are returning to yourself, one breath at a time.

Loving Yourself Even When You Feel Unlovable

There will be days when self-love feels far away. There will be days when shame rises, when memories sting, and when loneliness sits heavily on your chest. On those days, love yourself anyway. Wrap your arms around yourself. Speak softly to your own heart. Remind yourself that you deserve gentleness in every season.

Self-love does not ask for perfection. It asks for presence.

Love Defined — And Why Abuse Was Never Love

One of the most damaging effects of narcissistic abuse is how thoroughly it distorts the meaning of love. Survivors often leave these relationships believing that love requires endurance, self-erasure, emotional labor, or suffering. Many were told that control was care, jealousy was devotion, and cruelty was honesty.

Clarity begins with definition.

What Love Is

Love is patient, and love is kind.
It does not envy, and it does not boast.
It is not proud.
It does not dishonor others.
It is not self-seeking.
It is not easily angered, and it keeps no record

~ 1 Corinthians 13:4-8 NIV

Over time, the narrative I had carried about loss began to dissolve.

What I once believed was abandonment revealed itself as release.

Narcissists create burdens and baggage and they lose their blessing which is you.

I did not need to argue with that truth.

I only needed to stop carrying what was never mine.

CHAPTER TEN

THE UNTOUCHABLE ERA

The Woman You Become After Narcissistic Abuse

As mentioned earlier, there is a version of you that existed before distortion took hold. She did not disappear. She waited. What changes after narcissistic abuse is not her existence, but your relationship to her.

You begin to recognize her instincts again. You stop negotiating with what your body already knows. You stop making yourself smaller to preserve fragile peace.

This version of you is not created by suffering. She is revealed through it. She has walked through confusion, grief, withdrawal, and reclamation, and has emerged with a clarity that no longer requires reinforcement from others.

What once felt like breaking was the gradual dismantling of an identity shaped by survival rather than truth. Your pain was not random, but neither was it a destiny.

It marked a passage. You did not leave narcissistic abuse empty. You left carrying discernment shaped by lived experience, boundaries rooted in self-respect rather than fear, and an intuition that no longer asks permission to speak. What follows is often described as becoming untouchable, but that word does not refer to invulnerability or perfection. It describes a shift in orientation. You no longer organize your life around confusion. You no longer seek clarity from people who

benefit from your uncertainty. You no longer confuse intensity with intimacy or chaos with connection. You stop abandoning yourself in order to be chosen.

Becoming untouchable does not mean you are finished healing. It marks the end of healing that required endurance. You stop believing that love must cost you your safety. You trust your intuition earlier, not after it has been dismissed repeatedly. You recognize manipulation without needing to explain it. You sense misalignment without arguing yourself out of it. There are quiet changes that follow.

Your boundaries become less reactive and more factual. Your no does not require defense.

Your standards are no longer protection against harm. They are alignment with what sustains you. You stop outsourcing your reality to people who distort it.

The Laws of the Untouchable Woman

The woman who rises after narcissistic abuse does not return to who she was before. She lives by a different set of laws, shaped by clarity, self-trust, and experience earned at a cost.

Her no is a complete sentence. It does not require explanation, defense, or apology. Her boundaries are not walls built from fear. They are standards rooted in self-respect.

Her self-trust is no longer negotiable. She listens to her intuition when it speaks, not after it has been ignored for too long. She does not outsource her reality to people who distort truth or diminish her perception.

Her identity is unshakable. No one gets to rewrite her story again. She owns her name, her voice, her history, and the woman she is still becoming.

Her energy is treated as sacred. Access is given only to those who offer consistency, emotional maturity, respect, and peace. Everyone else is released without ceremony and without guilt.

Her future belongs to her. She no longer settles, shrinks, or sacrifices herself to preserve fragile dynamics. She builds a life that honors her nervous system, her values, and her truth.

Her understanding of love has changed. She no longer romanticizes suffering or bonds through brokenness. She knows that real love does not require self-erasure or emotional endurance.

Her past no longer frightens her. It informs her discernment. What once wounded her now strengthens her clarity. She is not afraid of darkness, because she learned how to become her own light.

As your relationship to the future changes, you stop shrinking to preserve dynamics that require self-erasure. You stop settling for proximity when what you want is presence. You begin making decisions that honor your nervous system, your values, and your truth.

Love becomes something you recognize by how safe it feels, not by how much you endure. The past no longer frightens you. It informs you.

What once wounded you sharpens discernment rather than fear. You are not drawn to darkness because you survived it. You are drawn to clarity because you no longer need to prove your strength.

Others may notice the change before you name it.

Your presence becomes quieter and more grounded. You do not perform confidence. You carry yourself differently because you are no longer bracing. This is not coldness. It is self-protection shaped by understanding. It is not arrogance.

It is wakefulness.

This is the Untouchable Era. It is not a declaration or a title. It is the internal certainty that nothing from the past gets to decide who you are now. The healing journey continues, but a threshold has been crossed.

What you survived did not break you, define you, or diminish you. It changed how you live, and it ensured that your silence will never again be required.

This is the era
she rises in.

What becomes possible after this clarity settles is explored further in the book that follows.

AFTERWORD

The healing journey continues, but you have crossed a threshold. You know now that what you survived did not break you, did not define you, and did not diminish you. It initiated you into a life that will never again require your silence.

If any part of this book helped you name what you lived through, your words may help another woman feel less alone. What you named here is not the end of your story. It is the moment your life begins to speak back.

BONUS CHAPTER

This bonus chapter is offered as an optional deep dive for readers who recognize a specific pattern within their experience of narcissistic abuse: relationships shaped by emotional immaturity, dependency, avoidance of responsibility, and the subtle transfer of adult roles onto the survivor.

Not every narcissistic relationship follows this structure. However, for many survivors, particularly those who are capable, nurturing, emotionally intelligent, and highly responsible, the harm did not come from overt cruelty alone, but from being slowly positioned as the emotional parent, stabilizer, or caretaker for a partner who refused to grow.

This chapter exists to name that pattern clearly, without diluting the emotional arc of the main book. It is designed to offer clarity, validation, and relief to readers who have long sensed that they were not simply "too much," but we were carrying the weight of someone who never fully matured.

You may read this chapter immediately, return to it later, or skip it entirely. Its purpose is not to instruct or diagnose, but to help you understand what you lived through, so that it no longer lives inside you unexamined.

IMPORTANT NOTE

This material is educational and reflective in nature. It is not a clinical diagnosis, nor a substitute for professional mental health or legal support. Every individual and relationship is unique. If you feel unsafe, overwhelmed, or at risk, please seek appropriate professional or crisis support in your area.

The Man-Child Narcissist: Emotional Immaturity, Peter Pan Syndrome, and Why Strong Women Are Targeted

Some narcissistic relationships are not built on domination alone. They are built on avoidance. Avoidance of responsibility. Avoidance of accountability. Avoidance of emotional adulthood.

Like any narcissist, the man-child appears charming, wounded, misunderstood, or simply "different" from other men. He may be emotionally expressive at first, quick to bond, eager to be cared for, and skilled at eliciting empathy. What looks like sensitivity, however, is emotional arrest.

The man-child has stopped developing somewhere earlier in life, often during childhood or early adolescence. Instead of growing forward, he has learned how to survive by attaching himself to women who can compensate for what he lacks.

Why Women Like You Are Targeted

The man-child narcissist does not choose randomly. He seeks women who are strong, organized, emotionally intelligent, responsible, empathic, and grounded. Their strength brings him the stability, emotional regulation he craves. It also allows him to escape consequences.

At first, this dynamic can feel flattering. He may defer to your judgment, rely on your decision-making, and describe you as the only person who truly understands him. Over time, however, the imbalance becomes exhausting. You are carrying emotional labor, logistical planning, financial stability, and relational repair, while he remains reactive, inconsistent, or avoidant.

One day, the realization hits: you are the only adult in the relationship and have been since the beginning.

Emotional Arrested Development

Emotionally immature narcissists may look simply irresponsible, but it goes much deeper than that. They are psychologically stuck. Adult intimacy requires accountability, self-reflection, and the ability to tolerate discomfort. These capacities threaten the man-child narcissist's fragile sense of self.

As a result, he avoids growth and transfers responsibility for any conflict and stress to you.

When faced with expectations, he may shut down, explode, deflect, blame, or retreat into distraction. In doing so he avoids his own unresolved issues—and distracting you from them as well.

Dependency Conditioning

Over time, the dynamic shifts. You stop expecting reciprocity. You stop asking for consistency. You start managing his moods, anticipating his reactions, and compensating for his lack of follow-through.

You may find yourself excusing his behavior to others, minimizing your own needs, or staying because you feel responsible for his well-being.

You were trained to believe that if you just supported him enough, stabilized him enough, or waited long enough, he would eventually become the man he promised to be.

That promise was the illusion.

Peter Pan Syndrome and the Fear of Adulthood

The Peter Pan narcissist fears adulthood because adulthood requires ownership of one's life. Commitment, long-term planning, financial responsibility, and emotional consistency all require maturity he has not developed.

Instead, he lives in the present, chases stimulation, avoids defining the relationship, keeps options open, and resists anything that limits his freedom. Ambiguity keeps him safe. Clarity threatens him.

You, however, need clarity to feel secure.

This mismatch is not because you are demanding. It is because you are an adult.

What This Says About You

If you recognize yourself in this dynamic, also recognize that your strengths have been exploited. No matter what he has done to make you feel that you are needy, naive, or weak. The fact is you have been a nurturing and stabilizing force in his life. You always showed up, even when he didn't. He simply didn't honor those qualities.

The Truth That Sets You Free

You cannot raise a grown man.
You cannot parent your partner.
You cannot save someone who refuses to grow.

And you do not need to sacrifice your adulthood so someone else can remain a child.

Understanding this pattern is not about anger. It is about release. Once you see that the relationship was never designed to mature, you stop blaming yourself for its collapse.

You were not asking for too much.
You were asking the wrong person.

And now, you know better.

Practicing Discernment

Discernment is the ability to see through narcissistic manipulation to the truth of a situation.

It is our compass in healing, guiding us to trust ourselves and recognize what serves our well-being.

> *I trust in my inner wisdom*
>
> *I see clearly, feel deeply, and respond with strength. I do not second-guess what I know to be true.*

Journal Prompts — Discernment

Who is the woman you refuse to shrink back into?

What parts of your power do you now reclaim unapologetically?

What does your untouchable era look and feel like?

Which boundaries define this new version of you?

What relationships no longer fit your healed identity?

What are you no longer available for ever again?

Discernment is the ability to notice what is present without forcing an explanation. It is not suspicion. It is not hypervigilance. It is awareness that remains steady.

Discernment pays attention to patterns. It tracks consistency over time. It does not treat intensity as evidence. It does not treat reassurance as a resolution.

Discernment recognizes that confusion is information. When something repeatedly feels unclear, unstable, or inconsistent, discernment does not rush to correct the feeling. It pauses and continues observing.

Discernment separates words from behavior. It notices when statements do not match actions. It notices when repair is promised but not practiced. It notices when apologies are repeated without change.

Discernment does not negotiate with the body. It considers physical cues as data, including tension, dread, and the sense of needing to monitor or manage. It does not interpret these cues as weaknesses. It treats them as feedback.

Discernment does not require certainty in the moment. It does not demand proof immediately. It allows time to confirm what repetition reveals.

Discernment does not require you to stay longer to be fair. It does not require you to make a case. It does not require you to override your own perception in order to preserve someone else's comfort.

Discernment is not harsh. It is protective. It is the capacity to remain aligned with reality before harm becomes the only form of clarity.

Sleep Deprivation as Control

Sleep Deprivation as Control Sleep Deprivation is one of the most effective and least recognized forms of psychological control in abusive relationships. It does not rely on raised voices or overt cruelty. It works quietly, over time, by eroding clarity, resistance, and self-trust.

For many survivors, rest did not disappear because of constant arguments. It became unavailable in subtle ways. Each time the body began to settle, something interrupted it.

A question framed as concern. A comment that could not wait until morning. A sudden need to talk about something. The disruptions were small enough to appear insignificant and frequent enough to leave the body depleted. By morning, exhaustion lingered without a clear cause. Thoughts moved more slowly. Boundaries softened. Words felt harder to find. Emotional reactions felt larger than expected.

Many survivors describe feeling apologetic without knowing why, assuming they were overreacting, assuming they were too sensitive, assuming they were the problem. Nothing about the behavior appeared extreme in isolation. There were no visible injuries and no single moment that explained the fatigue. What was harder to see was that rest itself had become incompatible with control. A well-rested partner can think clearly. A sleep-deprived person cannot.

Over time, the pattern created dependence. Fatigue made compliance easier. Confusion made explanation harder. Because the deprivation was often framed as intimacy or the need to resolve something important, resisting it felt selfish. Sleep was not withheld by force. It was negotiated away until exhaustion became the background state of the relationship.

One survivor later described nights when sleep became fragile rather than absent. Often, the interruption came at night. Sometimes he would wake her just to say good night, his voice pulling her back as her body was beginning to settle. Other times, each time her breathing

slowed and sleep approached, something interrupted it. The television volume turned up slightly. A voice breaking the quiet. A reminder that something needed to be discussed, framed as important and urgent.

Too tired to argue and wanting peace more than rest, she engaged. She listened. She responded. While she was still talking, answering what he had woken her to discuss, and his breathing began to slow. His responses faded.

Eventually, he fell asleep, sometimes quickly, his breath deepening into loud, steady snoring. She remained awake. Exhausted. Alert. Wanting to return to sleep but unable to do so. Her body stayed tense, as if rest were no longer permitted. Each interruption felt minor on its own.

Together, they prevented her nervous system from settling. Sleep became fragmented. Recovery became shallow. What appeared inconsequential accumulated quietly, night after night, training her body to remain vigilant even when nothing was happening.

By morning, she woke foggy and unsure, struggling to concentrate or explain why everything felt heavier than it should have. At the time, she believed the exhaustion was her own fault. She did not yet understand that being kept awake had softened her resistance. Fatigue had done what force never needed to.

This is how control embeds itself in the body. When sleep is disrupted consistently, perception weakens. When perception weakens, reality becomes negotiable. When reality becomes negotiable, control no longer needs to be enforced. Understanding this pattern does not require reliving it.

It offers context where there was once confusion. It explains how the body was compromised without suggesting that the survivor failed to protect themselves. Sleep deprivation was not incidental. For many, it was part of the environment.

A FEW WORDS ABOUT HEALING

There was a time in my life when I stayed in a relationship long after my inner voice told me that something was wrong. I take full accountability for that. I stayed through situations I should have left. I carried burdens that were never mine to hold. I gave more love, more understanding, and more chances than were ever returned.

There were moments of laughter and moments of sorrow, days filled with hope and long stretches of confusion. Throughout all of it, I kept trying. I believed that if I loved harder, gave more, or held on longer, something would eventually change. At the time, I did not understand that loving someone was not a problem. Loving the wrong person at the cost of myself was where I began to disappear.

Even in the pain, something was taking place that I could not see clearly then. I was not losing myself in the way I believed. I was being shaped through experience. In the aftermath of everything that fell apart, I began to recognize parts of myself that had gone quiet, including my sense of peace, my resilience, and a growing awareness that I deserved more than what I had accepted.

There came a point when fear stopped guiding every decision I made. I began choosing myself in small, deliberate ways. I started paying attention to my thoughts instead of fighting them. I learned to sit with discomfort without immediately trying to escape it. I released what I could not control and allowed life to unfold without forcing outcomes I could not sustain.

This process invited me to pause and look inward with honesty. I uncovered needs I had ignored and desires I had minimized. I learned how to be alone with myself without shame. In those quieter moments, I realized I was not breaking apart. I was changing.

I let go of the version of myself that survived by shrinking. I stopped trying to control what was never mine to manage. I learned to trust again, not blindly, but with awareness. I learned to see people more clearly, and I learned to see myself with greater honesty.

That relationship served a purpose because it revealed what I needed to learn. It showed me where I had been abandoning myself, and it gave me the opportunity to return. Nothing about the experience was wasted, even though it was painful. It brought me back to myself.

I no longer look outside of myself for validation in the way I once did. I understand now that clarity begins internally, and no one else should carry the responsibility of defining my worth. I am learning to live from that understanding, one choice at a time.

A RETURN TO SELF-LOVE, SELF-WORTH, AND GRATITUDE

This appendix is not here to inspire you for five minutes. It is here to give you practices you can return to, especially on the days you do not feel strong, confident, or certain.

Self-love, self-worth, value, and gratitude are not personality traits. They are habits of attention. They are choices you make in small moments that add up over time. If you have spent years adapting to other people, doubting yourself, or shrinking to keep the peace, these sections are a way back to yourself.

Section 1: Self-Love as a Daily Practice

Self-love is not indulgence. It is self-respect in action. It is how you speak to yourself when no one is watching, what you tolerate, what you repair, and what you refuse to keep carrying.

1. What Self-Love Means

Self-love is not a mood. It is a way of relating to yourself that changes your life.

Self-love looks like:

- Accepting yourself as a whole person, not a project you have to fix.
- Setting boundaries that protect your time, energy, and peace.
- Treating yourself with compassion instead of punishment.
- Taking your needs seriously, even when other people do not.

2. Challenge the Voice That Diminishes You

Most people do not struggle with self-love because they lack willpower. They struggle because they have internalized a voice that is critical, demanding, and impossible to satisfy.

Practice this:

- When you hear, "I'm not good enough," replace it with, "I am allowed to be human while I grow."
- When you hear, "I always mess up," replace it with, "I am learning, and learning includes mistakes."
- When you feel ashamed, remind yourself that shame is not guidance. It is a weight.

You are not your worst moment. You are the person who survived it and kept going.

3. Practice Self-Care That Nourishes You

Self-care is anything that helps you stay connected to yourself long-term, not just what makes you feel better for an hour.

Choose care that meets you where you are:

- Physical: eat in a way that supports your body, move in ways you can sustain, protect your sleep.
- Emotional: let yourself feel without rushing to fix, write what is true, ask for support when you need it.

- Mental: feed your mind with what expands you, not what drains you.
- Spiritual: return to what steadies you, whether that is prayer, stillness, nature, or meaning.

4. Set Boundaries Without Apologizing for Them

Loving yourself means you stop negotiating with what is hurting you.

Boundaries can sound like:

- I am not available for this.
- I will not explain myself repeatedly.
- I am leaving if the disrespect continues.
- I need time, and I will take it.

A boundary is not a threat. It is a decision.

5. Stop Comparing Yourself Into Self-Rejection

Comparison trains you to measure your life against what you cannot see clearly, which is why it never ends.

Instead, write down five things that make you you:

- The way you think.
- The way you notice details.
- The way you love people.
- The way you keep going.
- The values you refuse to abandon.

Self-love strengthens when you stop treating your uniqueness like a problem.

6. Forgive Yourself Without Erasing What Happened

Forgiveness is not pretending it did not matter. It is deciding you will not keep paying for it forever.

Try this:

- Name what you regret without dramatizing it.
- Take the lesson without carrying the shame.
- Make one choice today that aligns with the person you are becoming.

Section 2: Learning to Live from Your Worth

Self-worth is not something other people give you. It is what you decide is true about you, even when someone else does not recognize it.

1. Stop Seeking Validation as Proof

Validation feels good, but it cannot be the foundation. If your worth rises and falls based on other people's reactions, you will never feel settled.

Practice:

- Ask yourself what you think before you ask what they think.
- Make decisions based on values, not approval.
- Treat your inner voice like it matters, because it does.

2. Normalize Receiving What Is Good

Many people say they want love, respect, and stability, but their nervous system is more familiar with inconsistency.

Remind yourself:

- I am allowed to want better.

- I am allowed to receive better.
- I do not have to earn basic respect.

3. Identify and Replace the Beliefs That Keep You Small
Write down the belief, then challenge it with evidence.

Example:

- Belief: "I'm not good enough."
- Truth: "I have survived, adapted, learned, and I am capable."

Your beliefs shape your choices. Your choices shape your life.

4. Treat Yourself Like Someone You Love
If someone you loved was struggling, you would not speak to them with contempt. You would not call them lazy, dramatic, or too much.

Do the same for yourself:

- Speak with kindness.
- Offer encouragement.
- Protect yourself from harm, including emotional harm.

5. Choose Environments That Respect You
Self-worth grows faster when you stop staying where you are consistently diminished.

Start here:

- Distance yourself from people who punish you for having needs.
- Seek relationships where care is steady, not conditional.
- Pay attention to how you feel after you interact with someone.

6. Own Your Accomplishments Without Downplaying Them
Keep a simple record of what you do well. Not for ego, but for accuracy.

Start a "Wins Journal" and write:

- what you handled,
- what you completed,
- what you endured,
- what you chose differently this time.

Credit changes the way you see yourself.

Section 3: Knowing Your Value Without Comparison
Knowing your value is not ego. It is clarity. It is recognizing what you bring to the table and refusing to betray yourself to be chosen.

1. Reflect on Your Strengths and Contributions
Answer honestly:

- What do you do naturally that other people struggle to do?
- What perspective do you bring that is rare?
- Where have you made a difference, even quietly?

Value is often revealed in patterns, not compliments.

2. Stop Tolerating What Diminishes You
You cannot build confidence while staying in dynamics that require you to be smaller.

Truth to remember:

- If someone does not appreciate you, it is not proof you lack value.
- It is proof you are in the wrong environment.

3. Set Standards That Protect Your Life
Standards are not rules for other people. They are commitments to yourself.

Define what you will not accept in:

- relationships,
- work,
- friendships,
- your own self-talk.

Then follow through. Consistency is self-respect.

4. Speak Up for Yourself
Your voice matters even when it shakes.

Practice:

- Say what you need.
- Say what you mean the first time.
- Stop over-explaining to people committed to misunderstanding you.

5. Invest in Yourself With Intention
Investing in yourself is a form of self-trust.

Choose one:

- a book that challenges you in the right way,
- a course that builds a real skill,
- a practice that strengthens your discipline,
- a habit that improves your life in measurable ways.

Growth changes what you believe is possible for you.

Section 4: Practicing Gratitude Without Minimizing Your Life

Gratitude is not pretending everything is fine. It is learning to notice what is still here, even when something hurts. It is how you stay connected to your life while you are building a better one.

1. Keep a Daily Gratitude Journal

Write down three specific things each day. Keep them real.

- a moment of relief,
- a small kindness,
- something steady you often overlook.

On difficult days, do not search for something impressive. Choose something true.

2. Practice Presence in Short Moments

Gratitude grows when you stop rushing past your own life.

Try:

- one slow breath before you pick up your phone,
- noticing the temperature of your drink,
- sixty seconds of silence before you start the next task.

Presence is a return, not a performance.

3. Express Gratitude to Others

Say thank you with detail.

- Thank you for checking on me.
- Thank you for being consistent.
- Thank you for showing up when it mattered.

Clear gratitude strengthens safe connection.

4. Reframe Challenges Without Forcing Positivity

Instead of asking, "What is this teaching me?" when you are overwhelmed, ask something you can answer.

- What do I need right now?
- What boundary is this showing me?
- What is the next right step?

Reframing is perspective without denial.

5. Focus on What You Have Without Comparing Your Life

Comparison creates lack. Gratitude returns you to reality.

Self-love, self-worth, value, and gratitude are practices. Some days they will feel natural. Some days they will feel like effort. Both days count. What matters is that you keep returning to yourself with honesty, care, and self-respect.

HOLISTIC SELF-CARE: A GUIDE TO STRESS RELIEF AND SKINCARE ROUTINES

In today's fast-paced world, finding balance and prioritizing self-care is more important than ever. This guide offers practical tips for nurturing your body, mind, and spirit, while naturally weaving in ways to enhance your journey with our holistic self-care products.

Morning Self-Care Rituals

Starting your day with intention sets the tone for a calm and productive day. Try this simple morning routine:

- **Hydrate:** Begin with a glass of warm water infused with lemon to detoxify and wake up your system.

- **Mindful Moments:** Spend 5-10 minutes meditating or journaling to ground yourself.

- **Skincare Boost:** Cleanse your face with a gentle, natural cleanser to refresh your skin. Follow up with Hydrating Rosewater Mist to lock in moisture and promote a radiant glow.

Midday Stress Relief

As the day progresses, stress can creep in. Combat it with these tips:

- **Stretch Breaks:** Take 5-minute breaks to stretch and release tension in your shoulders and neck.

- **Aromatherapy On-the-Go:** Keep a small roller of Essential Oil. Roll it onto your wrists or temples when you're feeling overwhelmed. The soothing notes of lavender and chamomile can help center you.

- **Mini Mindfulness Practice:** Pause to take three deep breaths, inhaling through your nose for a count of four, holding for four, and exhaling through your mouth for four. This simple practice resets your nervous system.

Evening Wind-Down Routine

Your nighttime routine should signal to your body that it's time to rest and rejuvenate:

- **Unplug:** Turn off screens at least 30 minutes before bed to reduce blue light exposure.

- **Skincare Ritual:** Remove the day's impurities with a Gentle Botanical Cleanser, followed by nourishing a Rejuvenating Night Serum. Massage the serum into your skin using gentle upward motions for added relaxation.

- **Relaxation Soak:** Treat yourself to a warm bath infused with Herbal Bath Soak. The soothing blend of Epsom salts, lavender, and calendula relaxes sore muscles and prepares your mind for restful sleep.

Weekend Deep-Care Practices

Use your weekends to deepen your self-care routine and reconnect with yourself:

- **DIY Facial:** Treat your skin to a rejuvenating facial using an Exfoliating Herbal Mask. Apply the mask, let it sit for 10-15 minutes, and rinse with lukewarm water for smooth, glowing skin.

- **Journaling or Reflection:** Take some time to reflect on your week and set intentions for the next. Use prompts like, "What brought me joy this week?" or "How can I show myself more love and care?"

- **Connect with Nature:** Spend time outdoors, whether it's a walk in the park or sitting in your garden.

The Power of Consistency

True self-care is about showing up for yourself *consistently*. Start small and build habits that support your well-being. Remember, it's not about perfection but progress.

By integrating moments of care into your day and using products designed to enhance your routines, you're investing in your overall health and happiness. You deserve this time to nurture yourself, and we're here to support you every step of the way.

What you named here is not the end of your story. It is the moment your life begins to speak back.

Recipes for Healthy Eating:

Recipes for domestic violence survivors focus on simplicity, nutrient density, and ease of preparation. Here are a few ideas:

Breakfast:

- **Smoothies:** Blend spinach, kale, frozen berries, Greek yogurt, and a scoop of protein powder for a nutrient-packed breakfast.

- **Overnight Oats:** Mix oats, chia seeds, almond milk, and berries, leave overnight in the fridge, and top with nuts and Manuka honey in the morning.

Lunch and Dinner:

- **Quinoa Salad:** Combine cooked quinoa with diced vegetables (like bell peppers, cucumber, and cherry tomatoes), black beans, avocado, and a light vinaigrette.

- **Grilled Chicken and Vegetables:** Marinate chicken breasts in olive oil, lemon juice, and herbs, then grill alongside a variety of colorful vegetables.

- **Vegetable Stir-Fry:** Stir-fry broccoli, bell peppers, snap peas, and tofu or chicken in a ginger-garlic sauce, served over brown rice or noodles.

- Snacks:

- **Greek Yogurt Parfait:** Layer Greek yogurt with fresh berries and a sprinkle of granola or nuts.

- **Homemade Trail Mix:** Combine mixed nuts, dried fruits, and a few dark chocolate chips for a satisfying snack.

Considerations:

- **Accessibility:** Ensure ingredients are readily available and affordable.

- **Safety:** If cooking facilities are limited, focus on no-cook or microwave-friendly options.

- **Variety:** Provide a range of flavors and textures to make meals more enjoyable and satisfying

Nervous System Support and Gentle Regulation

The experiences described throughout this book affect more than memory or emotion. They affect the body.

Long-term exposure to unpredictability, emotional volatility, manipulation, and threat conditions the nervous system to remain alert even after danger has passed. Many survivors notice this as shallow breathing, racing thoughts, difficulty sleeping, sudden waves of anxiety, or a persistent feeling of being on edge without an identifiable cause.

These responses are not signs of weakness or failure to heal. They are the body's attempt to protect itself after prolonged stress.

This appendix is included as a support, not a prescription. The practices described here are not requirements, solutions, or expectations. They are offered as options for moments when the body needs help settling, orienting to safety, or returning to the present.

You are not expected to use all of them. You are not expected to use any of them. Read through them only if it feels supportive to do so.

Healing does not require constant effort. Sometimes it begins with allowing the body to exhale.

Why Breath Matters After Trauma

Breathing patterns shift under stress. During prolonged emotional threat, the body often adapts by breathing shallowly, holding the breath, or remaining in a state of quiet bracing. These patterns can persist long after the situation has ended, even when the mind understands that it is safe.

Gentle breathwork communicates directly with the nervous system. It supports the parts of the body responsible for calming stress responses, reducing vigilance, and restoring equilibrium. Over time, repeated experiences of regulated breathing help the body relearn what safety feels like.

Breathwork does not erase memory or emotion. It simply gives the body another reference point besides alertness.

Box Breathing: Restoring Stability

Box breathing uses a steady, balanced rhythm to invite the nervous system into regulation.

To practice, inhale slowly for a count of four. Pause gently for a count of four. Exhale for a count of four. Pause again for a count of four before beginning the next cycle.

This pattern helps the body move out of urgency and into steadiness. Many survivors find it supportive during moments of anxiety, mental overload, or emotional escalation.

The 4–7–8 Breath: Releasing Tension

The 4–7–8 breath emphasizes a slow exhale, which supports the body's natural calming mechanisms.

Begin by inhaling through the nose for a count of four. Hold the breath for a count of seven. Exhale slowly through the mouth for a count of eight.

This technique is often helpful before sleep or during moments when the body feels restless or unable to settle.

Alternate Nostril Breathing: Restoring Balance

Alternate nostril breathing, also known as Nadi Shodhana, supports balance between the nervous system's activation and calming responses.

To practice, sit comfortably. Gently close the right nostril with the thumb and inhale through the left. Close the left nostril with the ring finger, release the right nostril, and exhale through the right. Then inhale through the right nostril, switch again, and exhale through the left.

This practice can be especially grounding after experiences of gaslighting or mental confusion, as it supports clarity and internal coherence.

The Long Exhale: Soothing Trauma Bond Cravings

Trauma bonds are maintained not only emotionally, but physiologically. When the body has adapted to cycles of intensity and relief, moments of longing or anxiety can arise even when the relationship has ended.

The long exhale technique involves inhaling gently through the nose for a count of three and exhaling through the mouth for a count of six.

Extending the exhale signals safety to the amygdala, the part of the brain responsible for threat detection. This technique can be used during moments of craving, agitation, or emotional discomfort.

Breath Counting: Returning to Presence

Dissociation is a common response to prolonged emotional stress. It can create a sense of disconnection from the body, the environment, or the present moment.

Breath counting supports reconnection.

Begin by inhaling for a count of one and exhaling for a count of two. Then inhale for a count of two and exhale for a count of three. Continue increasing the count gradually until the breathing feels steady and natural.

The focus required for counting anchors the mind, while the breath anchors the body.

These practices are not meant to replace therapy, medical care, or other forms of support. They are included because healing is not only cognitive or emotional. It is physiological.

You are not required to calm yourself perfectly. You are not required to regulate on command. The body learns safety gradually, through repeated experiences of gentleness rather than force.

Even small moments of ease matter. Over time, they accumulate.

RESOURCES

National Resources:

National Domestic Violence:

- Hotline: 1-800-799-SAFE (7233)
- Website: www.thehotline.org

National Coalition Against Domestic Violence (NCADV):

- Website: www.ncadv.org

RAINN (Rape, Abuse & Incest National Network):

- Hotline: 1-800-656-HOPE (4673)
- Website: www.rainn.org

State-Specific Resources:

For state-specific resources, each state typically has its own coalition or organization dedicated to domestic violence support. Here's how you can find them:

- **State Domestic Violence Coalitions**: Search for "[State] domestic violence coalition" or "[State] domestic violence resources". These organizations often maintain directories of local shelters, support groups, legal aid, and counseling services.

- **State Hotlines**: Many states have their own domestic violence hotlines. These can often be found through state government websites, local law enforcement agencies, or through a search engine query like "[State] domestic violence hotline".
- **Local Shelters and Support Services**: Contacting local law enforcement or social services can often provide direct referrals to shelters and other resources available in your community.

Additional Tips:

- **Emergency Services**: In immediate danger, call 911.
- **Legal Aid**: Many states offer legal aid services for domestic violence survivors. Check with local legal aid societies or bar associations.
- **Counseling and Support Groups**: Hospitals, community health centers, and mental health organizations often provide counseling services or can refer you to support groups.

Hotlines and Helplines:

National Domestic Violence Hotline (USA): 1-800-799-SAFE (7233) or text LOVEIS to 22522

- Website: TheHotline.org

National Coalition Against Domestic Violence (USA):

- Website: NCADV.org

Shelters and Safe Houses:

Women's Shelters Directory (USA):

- Website: WomensShelters.org

Legal and Counseling Services:

Legal Aid (varies by location):

- Provides legal assistance for domestic violence survivors.

Counseling and Support Services:

- Local community centers, hospitals, or mental health clinics often provide counseling and support groups.

Online Resources and Information:

Love Is Respect:

- Website: LoveIsRespect.org

Rape, Abuse & Incest National Network (RAINN) (USA):

- Website: RAINN.org

Financial Assistance:

Local Government and Non-profit Organizations:

- Many offer financial assistance or grants for domestic violence survivors.

Safety Planning and Emergency Assistance:

Safety Planning Tools:

- Available through most domestic violence hotlines and shelters.

Emergency Services:

- In immediate danger, call emergency services (911 or equivalent).

ABOUT THE AUTHOR

Sharelle Ellis is a writer, entrepreneur, and survivor of narcissistic abuse. Her work is shaped by the realization that a relationship which appeared to be loving could gradually distort her understanding of herself and her own perceptions.

She began writing when she realized there were experiences she had lived through but did not yet have language for. Writing became a way to bring clarity to what had been minimized, denied, or reframed, and to name realities that are often difficult to articulate in real time. Her work is informed by lived experience with emotional manipulation and domestic violence, and by the long process of understanding how those dynamics take hold.

As the founder of Holistic Selfcare Lounge and Warrior In Restoration, Sharelle Ellis creates healing products and resources grounded in lived experience. Her work is designed for women who feel worn down, overstimulated, or disconnected from themselves, offering healing products that support balance, grounding, and restoration within everyday life.

She writes for women who are trying to understand themselves again after years of questioning their own perceptions.